Being Respectful

A Book About Respectfulness

by Mary Small   illustrated by Stacey Previn

PICTURE WINDOW BOOKS
Minneapolis, Minnesota

Thanks to our advisors for their expertise, research, and advice:

Bambi L. Wagner, Director of Education
Institute for Character Development, Des Moines, Iowa
National Faculty Member/ Trainer,
Josephson Institute of Ethics - CHARACTER COUNTS!sm
Los Angeles, California

Susan Kesselring, M.A., Literacy Educator
Rosemount-Apple Valley-Egan (Minnesota) School District

Editorial Director: Carol Jones
Managing Editor: Catherine Neitge
Creative Director: Keith Griffin
Editor: Jacqueline A. Wolfe
Story Consultant: Terry Flaherty
Designer: Joe Anderson
Page Production: Picture Window Books
The illustrations in this book were created with acrylics.

Picture Window Books
5115 Excelsior Boulevard
Suite 232
Minneapolis, MN 55416
877-845-8392
www.picturewindowbooks.com

Printed in the United States of America.

Library of Congress Cataloging-in-Publication Data
Small, Mary.
Being respectful / by Mary Small ; illustrated by Stacey Previn.
p. cm. — (Way to be!)
Includes bibliographical references and index.
ISBN 1-4048-1053-6 (hard cover)
1. Respect for persons—Juvenile literature.
2. Respect—Juvenile literature. I. Previn, Stacey. II. Title. III. Series.
BJ1533.R42S63 2006
179'.9—dc22   2005004274

Showing respect means caring how a person feels. Showing respect means doing things that show another person you think they are important.

Treating people with respect makes them, and you, feel good. You can show respect for other people, for yourself, and even for the world.

There are lots of ways to show respect.

These two teams high-five after the game.

They are showing respect.

Tamara happily *sets* the table
for her family at dinner.

She is showing respect.

Before the ball game starts, the crowd stands and removes their hats while "The Star-Spangled Banner" is sung.

They are showing respect.

Christine takes Muffy out of the room when her uncle comes to visit because he is allergic to cats.

She is showing respect.

Joe takes care of himself by bathing, studying, eating healthy food, and getting plenty of rest.

He is showing respect for himself.

Katie holds the door open
for her grandmother.

She is showing respect.

15

While playing in the yard, Mike is careful not to step on the flowers.

He is showing respect.

Josh invites everyone to be a part of the group.

He is showing respect.

Sam is sure to be home when his parents expect him.

He is showing respect

Caroline is always sure to thank the lunch server for her food.

She is showing respect.

At The Library

Loewen, Nancy. *Treat Me Right! : Kids Talk About Respect.* Minneapolis: Picture Window Books, 2003.

Riehecky, Janet. *Respect.* Mankato, Minn.: Capstone Press, 2005.

Schuette, Sarah L. *I Am Respectful.* Mankato, Minn.: Pebble Books, 2003.

On the Web

FactHound offers a safe, fun way to find Web sites related to this book. All of the sites on FactHound have been researched by our staff. www.facthound.com

1. Visit the FactHound home page.
2. Enter a search word related to this book, or type in this special code: 1404810536
3. Click the FETCH IT button.

Your trusty FactHound will fetch the best Web sites for you!

Index

Look for all of the books in the Way to Be! series:

Being Fair: A Book About Fairness

Being a Good Citizen: A Book About Citizenship

Being Respectful: A Book About Respectfulness

Being Responsible: A Book About Responsibility

Being Trustworthy: A Book About Trustworthiness

Caring: A Book About Caring